The History of Angels

One Message Many Faces

The History of Angels

One Message Many Faces

By

Bill Dale

Project Editor: Gail Hamrick

Willitts Designs
Petaluma, California

Dedication:

This book is dedicated to my wife,
Sherri, my daughter, Sarah, and our new son, Bradley.

Published by
Willitts Designs
© 1991 William Dale
Illustrations © 1993 Charles S. Pyle

ISBN: 0-9624693-4-3
Printed and bound in Hong Kong

Contents

Preface

Angels reside in the invisible and unknowable world, a unique dimension the human race can scarcely understand. Their existence in that celestial sphere is, and always has been, difficult to prove. Belief in angels, therefore, is a matter of faith.

The sacred scriptures of Judaism, Christianity, and Islam are filled with references to angels. These divine beings deliver mandates of God, announce special events, protect the faithful, punish adversaries, glorify God, and console believers. They also intercede for humanity, rejoice over repentant sinners, attend prayerful souls, escort the deceased to heaven, and participate in the final judgment.

However, when John sought to worship at the feet of an angel, he was told "You must not do that! I am a fellow servant . . . Worship only God." (Revelation 22:8) Angels, with all their mystical powers, are not Gods! They do not possess all of God's attributes nor can they control the human intellect or will. An angel can only interact with the human soul, and thus influence human sense and imagination.

But what form do these beings assume? Our perception of an angel is that of a winged human, yet there is very little scriptural basis for this image. Saint Thomas Aquinas reasoned that angels could assume whatever form they chose, and Martin Luther described angels as "spiritual creatures created without a body by God." Philo Judaeus, a Jewish philosopher, believed that the "human soul converts impressions of God into acceptable physical angelic forms," a form "the human soul could understand." In other words, the individual determines the shape and form of the angel.

In 1990, during an inspirational weekend experience called The Walk to Emmaus, I saw old friends from a profoundly new perspective. For a split second, God's message emanated from the souls of my friends and radiated like an unmistakable beacon of inspirational light, as though angels had momentarily taken their form. In my circumstance, God's message was wrapped in the cultural clothing of my friends. For other people, angels manifest themselves in different cultural forms.

The evolution of these forms is the topic of this book.

Bill Dale

Bill Dale

June 18, 1993

Introduction

O ur perception of an angel as a beautiful winged human flows from the imaginations of ninth through seventeenth century artists. To understand where these artists derived this image, thus narrowing Western civilization's perception of angels, we must examine religious history.

Ancient history is replete with images of winged messengers who reside in the celestial world and function as guardians of the faithful. In the powerful imagery of these ancient civilizations is found the basis for the winged human form in angelic art.

During the three thousand years before the Christian Era, when mythological beings still ruled the world, winged divinities played important roles in the religions of Egypt, Assyria/Babylonia, Persia, Greece, and Rome. From these cultures sprung such diverse subjects as the Egyptian Isis, an exemplary mother; the Assyrian Genie, a guardian spirit; and the Persian Mithra, light for humanity in times of darkness and evil.

Growing from these influences, classical Greek civilization provided a foundation for later philosophy, literature, art, and politics. The influence of Greek culture on both Judaism and Christianity cannot be overstated. Nike, because she is less godlike and more a messenger, provided a model for later physical depictions of angels interacting with humans.

Classical Greek portrayals of winged creatures became popular with the Romans, and therefore affected early Christian thought in Southern Europe. The Goths, who dominated Northern Europe at that time, remained isolated during the early Christian centuries and retained religious themes based in primitive superstitious beliefs. Even after their forced conversion to Christianity, the Goths preserved their ancestors' beliefs in art and literature, with many components of their violent and barbaric past.

Without question, the most dramatic interpretations of angels occurred during this period when converted pagans presented the biblical angel in the cultural clothing of their past beliefs. Stories of the biblical angels' abilities to summon earthquakes and floods and annihilate whole armies fascinated the Gothic people. In particular, they were consumed by the dramatic stories of Gabriel at the Annunciation and Michael at the final judgment. Reflected in these portrayals is the hope of the Gothic people in the face of war and disease.

It was during the Renaissance, however, that the interpretation of angels as winged human forms reached its zenith. Fusing pagan imagery with the biblical angel, the Renaissance artist created portrayals that remain permanently ingrained in the collective memory of contemporary society. More than any other generation, these artists managed to deliver God's message in a form that the human soul could understand. Their images were not only appreciated for their artistic beauty, but worshipped for their holiness.

Some of the most important subjects of the Renaissance period were the guardian angels, musical angels, and cherubs.

Overlapping the final years of the Renaissance, and reaching into modern times, was an era of powerful new religious thought as well as great scientific inquiry. The first is epitomized in the Protestant Reformation; the second is reflected in the growth of scientific disciplines. Although neither of these influences was comfortable with angels, artists continued to interpret the messengers of God for the common people who still needed them in their daily lives.

During the Reformation, Renaissance imagery of angels celebrating and protecting human life was replaced with a more sober and reflective portrayal. The angel was seen conveying God's message in times of fear, as in the dramatic interpretation of the angel comforting Jesus in the Garden of Gethsemane. The sensitive topic of death was also addressed, but was softened by the portrayal of an angel bearing the soul of the righteous to heaven. In a time when many were seeking answers to difficult questions, the human soul once again grasped God's message in an acceptable angelic form.

Throughout religious history, the angel survives, evolving and adapting to each cultural circumstance. This evolution continues into contemporary times. The book's final portrayal depicts our angelic double struggling to save the human soul. Presented is the angel who resides inside all of us. This winged subject wears the cultural clothing of our moral conscience and serves as our guide, protector, and instructor on our earthly journey. This angel, our angelic double, is deep rooted in religious history and best exemplifies the cultural attire of God's message in the twentieth century.

Isis
Egyptian Influence on Angelic Art

2000 B.C.E.–30 B.C.E.

I sis kneels on a sarcophagus, her beautiful face lifted toward the heavens. In her left hand rests an ankh, a "token of life" bestowed on the Egyptian kings by the gods. Her right hand holds out a sistrum, a musical instrument that paralyzes the powers of darkness. Her mighty wings protect a deceased believer. For two thousand years this powerful image of eternal life reigned across Egypt and the Mediterranean, promising her followers salvation and regeneration after death.

The winged human form was first elevated to a position of majesty by the Egyptians, and the goddess Isis was one of the earliest mythological beings to wear divine wings. Those who followed Isis believed she had taught their ancestors how to grind flour, spin clothes, weave baskets, and cure illnesses. She was credited with introducing the custom of marriage and establishing the traditional role of mother and wife, thereby becoming the model for all Egyptian women.

When Alexander the Great conquered Egypt in 331 B.C.E., Greek culture completely Hellenized the cult of Isis. The Greeks worshipped Isis, and formed small communities across Asia Minor to practice the cult. After the Romans conquered Egypt in 30 B.C.E., the cult spread over the entire Mediterranean basin. Only when Christianity became the dominant religion did the cult of Isis vanish.

Yet the practices of the Isis cult impacted many generations and surrounding cultures. Many of her religious symbols are still part of religious traditions. Isis' followers confessed their sins; her priests were fishermen; a ladder symbolized spiritual advancement; the anchor symbolized security; grain separated from the chaff represented the cleansing of the soul; the palm represented victory and rebirth.

Although Isis was not an angel, her beautiful image strongly influenced future artists' depictions and perceptions of the winged human form.

The Benevolent Genie
Assyrian/Babylonian Influence on Angelic Art

⊷ ⊟◈⊟ ⊶

1100 B.C.E.–250 B.C.E.

"Now the land of Israel was filled with Assyrian troops . . .
besieging Samaria, the capital city of Israel. Finally, in the
ninth year . . . Samaria fell and the people of Israel were exiled
to Assyria." (II Kings 17:5)

After the decline of Sumeria in 2000 B.C.E., the tribes of Mesopotamia were consolidated into two great empires—Babylonia to the South and Assyria to the North. These two powerful kingdoms ultimately destroyed and subsequently controlled the Jewish nation. Sumerian and Semitic gods were blended by the Assyrians and ranked according to importance, influence, and power. Thus was created the winged Benevolent Genie who for over one thousand years figured prominently in Assyrian art.

The Genie's position in the celestial hierarchy and his functions within that hierarchy closely resemble those of angels from the sacred text. Like angels, the Genie reported to higher authorities, played a major role in the people's daily lives, acted as a guardian/protector of the Assyrian warrior, defended the individual from evil powers, appeared in either spiritual or physical form, and bestowed divine favor on the believer. It is evident that the Genie played a major role in the daily life of the Assyrian.

Because the Assyrians believed that the universe was run by "humanlike" beings with supernatural powers, the winged Genie was portrayed in the fashion codes of the period. Clothing, hair, and beards were used by the Assyrians to measure rank and status; the winged Genie was one of the most influential members of their society.

Our version of the Benevolent Genie, therefore, finds him in regally adorned clothing with beard intricately curled and braided. With one strong hand he lifts a pail that contains fluid from the sacred tree. Assyrians believed the tree united this world with the dwelling place of the gods above. His other hand grasps a pine cone with which he sprinkles holy water on all entrants to the monarch's palace. This powerful water also purifies and immunizes the king from the influences of evil powers.

⊷ ⊟◈⊟ ⊶

Mithra

Persian Influence on Angelic Art

— ❈ —

2000 B.C.E.–250 C.E.

The Persian culture had a profound impact on angelic art. Zoroaster, a Persian religious leader, introduced a one-god religion in which he transformed the Babylonian and Assyrian gods into archangels. Under Zoroaster, Persia slowly developed a religious system that employed the forces of light to protect the human soul from the forces of darkness. One of their mightiest protectors was the archangel Mithra, who embodied light and purity.

Mithra possessed strength, knowledge, and wisdom and was the source of truth and order. He guaranteed truthful followers worldly success, victory in battle, and joy in the after world. As angelic mediator between heaven and earth, Mithra served as the judge and preserver of the world.

Over the centuries, Mithra has been depicted many different ways, some with ten thousand eyes and others with a lion's head. We portray him in one of his most impressive forms, carrying a club (so sacred it deserves veneration) and a mace (a ceremonial weapon that represents Mithra's duty to fight against the powers of evil). Issuing from the globe at his feet and entwined around his mighty chest is a serpent that represents the regeneration of life. Its coils signify stages of purification and the ascent of the soul. Mithra's cape is adorned with the signs of the zodiac denoting the power of the stars.

For two hundred years Mithra competed against other religions for the soul of humankind. Followers of Mithra preached that he was the incarnation of eternal light, and stated that Mithra's birth was witnessed by many shepherds. They discussed the many good deeds he accomplished on earth, his return to heaven after a last supper with friends, and his ultimate return to participate in the last judgment.

Other religions ultimately prevailed against the Mithra cult, however, because Mithra was unforgiving. He made no attempt to convert sinners by peaceful means and cruelly punished those who sinned. Nevertheless, this Persian system based on one god with many archangels in conjunction with the winged visual imagery of Mithra elevated the status and roles angels would play in religious history.

— ❈ —

Nike
Greek Influence on Angelic Art

335 B.C.E.–700 C.E.

Isis' beauty, the Genie's ability to descend to earth in mortal or divine form, and Mithra's qualities of truth and justice are all combined in Nike, the Greek goddess of victory. With a laurel wreath in one hand, a sacred scroll listing heroes of the past in the other, and her powerful wings spread wide, Nike descends to earth to crown a victor.

Greek civilization owed much to the Egyptian, Assyrian, and Persian cultures that preceded it, but it was the Greek philosophers who offered Western civilization the first picture of personal inner development. In their civilization is the beginning of psychology as well as philosophy, and a new subjectivity in spiritual matters.

The ancient Greeks depicted many winged subjects in their art and architecture, and Nike was one of these. All Greek competitors dreamed of being crowned as victors by Nike who became the main motivator for the finest and best citizens.

Nike, the lovely winged feminine model, represents a defining point in the history of angelic art. Her physical beauty strongly influenced the Renaissance artists' interpretation of the biblical angel. From her image came bodies that were luminous; wings that were emblematic of spirit, power, and swiftness; and the development of a halo that symbolized sanctity. Early depictions of angels wore Nike's Grecian/Roman tunic to lend an air of dignity, her white clothing to symbolize divine light and purity, and her diadem to represent divine power.

As Western civilization established the winged human as the acceptable angelic form, the image of an angel evolved into more dramatic portrayals. The images created by Gothic and Renaissance artists represent the ultimate religious experience for believers searching for spiritual answers to human problems. These artists owe a debt of gratitude to Nike, their model from Greek mythology.

The Archangel Michael

Gothic Interpretation of Michael at the Last Judgment

—◦—❧◆❧—◦—

1100 C.E.–1500 C.E.

He is the angel of repentance, righteousness, mercy, and sanctification. He is the celestial high priest, protector and advocate of Israel and keeper of the heavenly keys. Dead Sea Scrolls call him the Prince of Light. Michael, which means "who is like God," is the greatest of all angels in Jewish, Islamic, and Christian religions.

Michael is an archangel concerned not with the individual so much as with the defense of the entire human race. Daniel 12:1 states, "at that time Michael the mighty angelic prince who stands guard over your nation will fight the satanic forces." Some stories imply that he presides over humankind and chaos and is the protector to be invoked while awaiting the outcome of the great combat of the Apocalypse.

Michael is referred to in the Bible on ten separate occasions performing four functions: He fights Satan, rescues the souls of the faithful from the power of the devil, brings the soul to judgment, and is patron of the church. Sometimes Michael is identified as the angel who stayed the hand of Abraham on Isaac; others say he is the angel who fought for the body of Moses. Still other legends credit him with being the one who told Eve to plant a branch of the tree of knowledge on Adam's grave—the branch that grew into the tree King Solomon removed to the Temple Garden then later discarded into the pool at Bethseda. This same tree eventually was fashioned into Jesus' cross.

When Christian conversion came to the Goths, a warrior people of Northern Europe, they especially venerated Michael. A people who continually faced anxieties hastened by war and disease, the Goths believed the final battle was near. They accepted their artists' renditions of the Revelation as literal interpretations.

Gothic artists depicted Michael as a strong and handsome man fitted in armor, carrying a shield and a sword, an image that has its origin in Ephesians 6:11 that states, "put on the whole armor of God." Our portrayal of Michael follows this image, with the armor a symbol of chivalry, the shield his protection against evil, and the sword representing the military virtues of power, strength, and bravery.

—◦—❧◆❧—◦—

The Angel Gabriel
Gothic Interpretation of Gabriel at the Annunciation

1100 C.E.–1500 C.E.

Gabriel, which means "hero of God," is found in Jewish, Christian, and Islamic religions. Jewish legends say he is one of the seven angels who stand by God's throne. He is credited with destroying Sodom and Gomorra, and with coming to the rescue of Israel by destroying the Assyrian army. In Islamic literature Gabriel represents the spirit of truth; it was he who revealed the Koran to Mohammed. In biblical scripture Gabriel delivers visions, reveals their meaning, and provides wisdom and understanding to old and new testament characters.

Still other legends and traditions believe Gabriel to be the ruler of paradise, giving him authority over the seraphim and cherubim and all other heavenly figures of power. He is also seen as one who brings the message of resurrection, mercy, vengeance, death, and revelation. Recent traditions see him blowing the horn at doomsday, summoning the righteous to their eternal inheritance.

This angelic figure is also tied to the message of the gift of God's special child. In this context Gabriel is the angel of the Annunciation and is seen as the chief ambassador to humanity. It was Gabriel who came to Mary and said, "Don't be frightened for God has decided to wonderfully bless you!" (Luke 1:30–31)

Our image is based on the Gothic artists' interpretation of this important moment in religious history. Gabriel is portrayed as handsome and richly robed. A glowing halo encircles his head; beautiful colored wings rest peacefully behind him. In his hand he holds a lily that is a symbol of the Immaculate Conception of Christ, the miracle he was chosen to announce.

Just as the Goths were fascinated with the power of Michael, they were intrigued with the stories of Gabriel. Gabriel's message delivered to Mary gave them hope in hopeless times. The artistic portrayals of the Annunciation gave them strength to continue their spiritual journey, even during one of human history's most oppressive periods.

The Guardian Angel Raphael
Renaissance Interpretation of the Guardian Angel

—————— ⧉◆⧉ ——————

1300 C.E.–1500 C.E.

The Renaissance began in Italy in the fourteenth century and continued for about two hundred years. It was a transitional period in Europe, between medieval and modern times, and was marked by a humanistic revival of classical influence. Legends and folklore, art and theology, mixed with Renaissance religious thought, expanded the roles of angels. Artists portrayed angels, the physical manifestation of God's word, performing many roles and functions, among which was that of spiritual guardian.

Guardian spirits are deep rooted in religious history. In most religions, past and present, these guardian forces serve to protect, direct, and guide us on our path through life. They are found in ancient Persian beliefs and in the Hebrew Kabbal, whose guardian spirit was known as Sandalphon. Solomon, it is said, was guarded by hordes of angels. Psalm 90 states, "for he hath given his angels charge over thee, to keep thee in all thy ways," which caused a fourth century bishop of Milan to believe that servants of Christ could pray and summon invisible beings for protection. Thomas Aquinas held that each person is assigned an angel to assist on the journey to heaven.

The spiritual guardian story that most intrigued the people of the Renaissance was that of the Apocrypha character Tobias who, as a young man, is accompanied on a journey to Persia by an older man. When in Persia the older man reveals himself as the angel Raphael.

Raphael, which means "divine healer," is an angel who watches over all humanity, guiding the spirits of the people. In some folklore Raphael is described as a Seraph—a six-winged angel that resides nearest to God. Others believe Raphael defended God's decision to create humankind, and he guards the tree of life in the Garden of Eden.

Most Renaissance illustrations show Raphael traveling with a staff, his feet adorned with sandals. The staff carries divine powers, represents authority, sovereignty, legality and judicial power. He carries a wallet with a shoulder strap and a gourd filled with water, symbolizing the brevity and frailty of life. Our portrayal reveals Raphael with his hand resting gently on the shoulder of Tobias. The child, hat in hand, listens attentively to the instructions delivered by his guardian angel for he knows that these instructions will guide him safely through the dangerous roads ahead.

Once again God's message is delivered in a form the soul could understand, a form that offered the peasantry care, protection, understanding, and direction.

—————— ⧉◆⧉ ——————

Musical Angels
Musical Influence on Angelic Art

・—◦◼◈◻◦—・

1300 C.E.–1600 C.E.

"Harmony, from heavenly harmony
This universal frame began
From harmony to harmony
Through all the compass of the notes it ran
The diapason closing full in man"

Two glorious angels clothed in colorful Renaissance-era garb, their smiling faces turned heavenward, sing the song for St. Cecelia's Day. The beautiful melody echoes through the skies in celestial celebration.

Music has always been associated with prayer. In the beginning it was considered a sacred art whose origin was ascribed to the supernatural world. In nearly all mythologies, music was given to humanity by the gods. It was truly the language of prayer and communication between human beings and spirits, evolving from a force that possesses the person to one that creates an order conducive to meditation and reflection.

Throughout history, ample evidence of the importance of music is found. In Assyrian texts and art we see them reminding worshipers that the gods appreciated singing during the performance of sacred rites. Persians chanted musical modes to communicate with the spiritual world. The Greek mythological Muses inspired music and the divine creative power. Islam had an angel of music, Israfil, who glorified Allah with his trumpet. Jews and Christians refer to Jubal as the first musician and the inventor of the harp and the flute. (Genesis 4:21)

During the Renaissance, however, inspirational music reached its zenith becoming an essential part of daily life. Every person of culture was expected to improvise music. In this atmosphere of musical euphoria, Dante elevated the status of the musical angel. His writings suggested that the symbols of God's beautiful order, singing angels, were necessary to maintain the cosmological order. Dante believed that without musical angels, God's creation would disintegrate.

・—◦◼◈◻◦—・

Cherubs
Renaissance Interpretation
of Cherubic Art

— ✦ —

1300 C.E.–1600 C.E.

The word cherub evolved from the Assyrian language and is part of Jewish, Christian, and Islamic traditions. Some of these traditions say cherubim are winged creatures with human faces who reside near God. They are blessed with wisdom and knowledge so they can convert God's complicated design into workable human plans.

In Old Testament scriptures, cherubim, which means "fullness of God's knowledge," stand at the entrance of the Garden of Eden and reside in the Hebrew Holy Temple. The Bible and Talmud equate cherubs with "living" chariots used to rescue God's faithful. And Muslim traditions say that the cherubim were formed from Michael's tears shed over the sins of the faithful.

The Renaissance perception of cherubs originates from a reinterpretation of a Hebrew word meaning "childlike." From this interpretation resulted the use of Greek and Roman images of childlike subjects, such as Eros and Cupid, to depict cherubic angels. These angels functioned as guides and directors of young children, representing a relationship of love between God and humankind. Possessing great wisdom, they bestow it on believers and dwell with people who are at peace with God. Christian folklore even has them serving as playmates for Baby Jesus.

The Renaissance interpretation of the Old Testament cherubim gives us further proof that the human soul converts images of God's messenger into acceptable angelic forms. Our cherubs celebrate the birth of Christ, announcing the wondrous entry of the promised new life into the world with the purity of innocence and the grace of beauty. We have taken this innocence and beauty one step further than the artists of the Renaissance by allowing our cherubs to take on ethnic qualities, thereby expanding the acceptable angelic form to fit into our world.

— ✦ —

The Garden of Gethsemane

The Angel's Role in Times of Fear

—•—❈❖❈—•—

1600 C.E.–1900 C.E.

In the Garden of Gethsemane, on the night of his betrayal, "an angel from heaven appeared and strengthened Jesus for he was in such agony of spirit that he broke into a sweat, with great drops of blood." (Luke 22:43) The angel's hands tenderly cradle his head and her graceful wings wrap around him to strengthen him in his resolve of "Not my will, but thine!" Jesus' hands are outstretched in supplication, and God sends comfort and support embodied as an angel.

Fear, a painful emotion that can be more powerful than a physical blow, is referred to in the Bible more than five hundred times. The angel plays an important role in times of fear, as is dramatically portrayed in the story of Jesus in the Garden of Gethsemane. This poignant story of Jesus' tremendous fear and the angel's comfort was quickly accepted by congregations struggling to define their beliefs in a time when they were being questioned and attacked on all sides.

In the seventeenth century, the powerful influence of angels incurred some major blows from the religious and scientific communities. Catholic church leaders became concerned with the formidable religious stature of angels, so eliminated their message-carrying capabilities. The new religious movements founded by Martin Luther and John Calvin downgraded the angel's biblical significance, abolishing any symbols that cluttered the image of God as the all-powerful being.

At this same time, the scientific revolution was occurring. The scientific community questioned all that could not be empirically verified by the five physical senses; this included the existence of angels.

Yet the angel survived these forces because the peasantry still needed God's message embodied in an acceptable form. The oppressive force of fear was ever-present, and the populace searched for spiritual understanding of the roles their religion would play in their lives. Artists mirrored these concerns with dramatic visual interpretations of angels comforting, preparing, and strengthening the human soul. These portrayals delivered a much-needed message—Fear not, for I am with you.

—•—❈❖❈—•—

The Ascension of the Soul

Reformation Artists' Interpretation of Eternal Life

1600 C.E.–1900 C.E.

"The soul of man will not die for they are equal unto the angels
and are the children of God." (Matthew 22:30; Luke 20:36)

Tatian, a second century church father, wrote "of itself the soul is not immortal, but mortal . . . nevertheless, it is capable of not dying depending on its relation to God."

Death—the ultimate mystery. Is it an ending or a beginning? Should one rejoice at its coming or feel sorrow? And what is on the other side? These questions have been asked over and over again as humankind struggled to understand this greatest of all mysteries.

Emily Dickinson referred to death as "a wild night and a new road." This was the perception of the people in the Reformation period. Death began to be perceived as the final stage of growth, a function of life rather than a function of sin. At this time, the center of interest in humankind's destiny shifted from the final judgment at the end of time to the immediate judgment of the human soul. And a new understanding of death began to emerge.

The angel's role in death became a favorite subject of Reformation artists who depicted the battle between good and evil (symbolized by angels and demons) vying for a dead person's soul. Many paintings portrayed angels protecting the dying person's family while other angels defended and delivered the person's soul from evil.

In our representation a beautiful angel ascends to the heavens bearing a person's soul in her tender embrace. Following the tradition of Reformation artists, we have portrayed this soul as an infant to symbolize the new beginning in eternity for the believer. God's message delivered by the angel inspires, encourages, and motivates the dying person to win the last earthly battle, to accept the inevitability of death and the victory of new life that comes with it.

The Angelic Double
The Struggle to Save the Human Soul

A ccording to Hermas, an early Christian leader, "there are two angels with a man—one of righteousness, and the other of iniquity." The angel of righteousness was referred to as the soul's angelic double.

Early Christian Gnostics believed the angelic double was the soul's spiritual counterpart that sees the Father in heaven. St. Anthony saw his angelic double while starving to death in the desert; he appeared in a brackish pool and showed him how to obtain food. In Acts 12:15, Peter's friends could not believe that he had escaped from jail and therefore reasoned that the image they saw must be Peter's angelic double.

One of the strongest Biblical models of an angelic double is found in the story of Jacob in Genesis 32. Jacob, whose name means "deceiver," had deceitfully stolen his brother Esau's birthright. After escaping to a nearby land and becoming wealthy, he decided to return home. On the night before he encountered his brother, Jacob was visited by an angel with whom he wrestled throughout the night. According to scripture, "when the angel saw that he couldn't win the match, he struck Jacob's hip."

Although Jacob was injured, he would not release the angelic double until he was blessed. The blessing was a new name—Israel, meaning "he strives with God and is happy." Jacob, convinced that he had seen the face of God in wrestling with his angelic double, was transformed. He went on to become the father of the nation of Israel.

Our figure portrays Jacob's moment of unity with God. Jacob's refusal to release the angel's arm represents his determination to free his soul from worldly constraints. The chain symbolizes the "things of this world," such as fear, anger, and jealousy, that bind Jacob's soul to its worldly existence. In the angelic double is found the face of God directing Jacob toward more noble goals. The angelic double senses Jacob's determination and faith so assists him to ascend to a higher spiritual plane.

The spiritual journey to our angelic double is difficult. It starts as a seed of faith and begins to grow when we begin to listen for God's message carried on the wings of silence. This message may be delivered so simply we barely notice; it may be in a kind word or tender touch, in a child's smile or a destitute's hand. Regardless of the form the message takes, when we sense our angelic double we must make an effort to strengthen the revelation.

It is in this effort that most people fail. Many have heard the wings of silence calling from deep within their souls, but failed to nourish its message. Many have reached for their angelic double only to allow the web of earthly fears and desires to entrap them. Though no human being is blessed with all the attributes of an angel,

every person can serve as an angel by delivering God's message. A bishop of Skara said, "and a man also, so far as he receives heaven, . . . is an angel."

So just as that ancient match transformed "Jacob the deceiver" into "Israel, the one who wrestles with God and is happy," so contemporary spiritual struggles can transform deceivers into believers. Success depends only on our ability to grip the arms of our angelic doubles with the same faith and determination as Jacob. For those who are successful, the struggle to save their soul will be complete. They will be transformed into beacons of inspirational light to assist others in their spiritual struggle; they will be like angels delivering God's message.

I met some of these angels during my walk to Emmaus.

Epilogue

Edward B. Lindana in *Thinking in the Future Tense* stated "One of Life's most fulfilling moments occurs in that split-second when the familiar is suddenly transformed into the dazzling aura of the profoundly new." This occurred to me during an inspirational retreat, "Walk to Emmaus" in 1990.

Bibliography

Adler, Mortimer J. *The Angels & Us*, 1988.

Becatti. *The Art of Ancient Greece & Rome*, 1967.

Burnham, Sophy. *A Book of Angels*, 1990.

Buttrick, George A. & Kieth R. Crim, Ed. *The Interpreters Dictionary of the Bible*, 1962.

Campbell, Joseph & M.J. Abadie. *The Mythic Image*, 1981.

Carlyon, Richard. *A Guide to the Gods: An Essential Guide To World Mythology*, 1989.

Cavendish, Richard & Oswald Ling. *Mythology an Illustrated Encyclopedia*, 1980.

Christie, Yves. *The Art of the Christian World*, 1982.

Church, F. Forrester. *Entertaining Angels: A Guide to Heaven for Athiests & True Believers*, 1987.

Davidson, Gustiv. *A Dictionary of Angels: Including the Fallen Angels*, 1972.

Elliot, Alexander. *Myths*, 1976.

Elwood, Roger. *Angelwalk*, 1991.

Ferguson, John. *Encyclopedia of Mysticism & Mystery Religions*, 1976.

Fergusson, George. *Signs & Symbols in Christian Art*, 1959.

Friedman, Richard Elliot. *Who Wrote the Bible?* 1987.

Gilmore, D. Don. *Angels Angels Everywhere*, 1981.

Godwin, Malcolm. *Angels: An Endangered Species*, 1990.

Graham, Billy. *Angels*, 1991.

_____. *Angels: God's Secret Agents*, 1986.

_____. *Angels: God's Secret Agents* - Revised & Expanded, 1986.

_____. *Facing Death & The Life After*, 1987

Gray, John. *Near Eastern Mythology*, 1985.

Grimal, Pierre, Ed. *Larousse World Mythology*, 1965.

Guirand, Felex, Ed. *New Larousse Encyclopedia of Mythology*, 1974.

_____. *Larousse Encyclopedia of Mythology*, 1959.

Hennessy, John Pope. *Luca Della Robbia*, 1980.

Kantonen, T.A. *Life After Death*, 1975.

Lowrie, Walter. *Art in the Early Church*, 1969.

Lukonin, W.G. *Persia II*, 1967.

Macmillan Illustrated Encyclopedia of Myths & Legends, 1989

Madhloom, T.A. *The Chronology of Neo-Assyrian Art*, 1970.

Matthews, Boris, Tr. *The Herder Symbol Dictionary*, 1986.

Moolenburgh, H.C. *A Handbook of Angels*, 1990.

_____. *A Handbook of Angels: Reflections On Angels Past & Present &True Stories of How They Touch Our Lives*, 1991.

Murray, Aynsley & Harriet Georgiana Maria. *Symbolism of the East & West*, 1971.

Museum of Fine Arts, Boston. *And the Angels Sing*, 1991

Parrot, Andre. *Arts of Assyria*, 1961.

Potok, Chaim. *Wanderings-Chaim Potok's History of the Jews*, 1978.

Ronner, John. *Do You Have a Guardian Angel?* 1985.

Roth, Cecil & Geoffrey Wigoder, Ed. *Encyclopedia Judaica*, 1982.

Russel, Burton. *Satan: The Early Christian Tradition*, 1981.

Russel, John. *Persian Mythology*, 1985.

Sill, Gertrude Grace. *A Handbook of Symbols in Christian Art*, 1975.

Souchal, Francis. *French Sculptors of the 17th and 18th Centuries*, 1977.

Ward, Theodora. *Men and Angels*, 1969.

Warren, Rex. *Encyclopedia of World Mythology*, 1980.

Zaehner, Robert. *The Dawn & Twilight of Zoroastrianism*, 1961.

Glossary

Ankh: A cross with a loop at the top that was believed by ancient Egyptians to be a symbol of life and eternity.

Apocalypse: Literally the uncovering of events; by derivation a revelation and in the case of Christianity, the final revelation found in the biblical book by the name that details the final battle between good and evil.

Apocrypha: The fourteen books written during the period between the Old and New Testament books, approximately 200 B.C.E. to 100 C.E., usually placed between the Testaments in Roman Catholic Bibles, but generally omitted by Protestant Bibles as rejected as Holy Scripture during the Reformation.

B.C.E.: An abbreviation used to designate the period of time Before the Common Era, commonly referred to as B.C. or Before Christ by Christians.

C.E.: An abbreviation used to designate that period of time known as the Common Era, commonly referred to as A.D. (*anno Domini* or "in the year of the Lord") by Christians.

Cherubim: Angelic figures identified in Jewish literature, usually described as four-winged, four-faced creatures, whose role seems to be one of guarding sacred places.

Gothic: Refers to the Goths, inhabitants of Northern France and parts of Germany during the Middle Ages, whose isolated culture was marked by primitive, violent, barbaric, and superstitious beliefs, as Julius Caesar discovered in one of his excursions. Even after their conversion to Christianity, their art and literature often preserved components of this past. The term is applied then to a style of fiction characterized by the use of desolate or remote settings and macabre, mysterious, or violent incidents. Of course, it is also applied to the architecture and ideas that developed in this area in the period 100 to 1500 C.E.

Gnostics: Sect of Christians in the first two centuries who valued inquiry into spiritual truth as more important than faith. Most were declared heretical by the third century.

Hellenized: Acculturated to Greek ideas from the Greek's own name for their country.

Kabbal: A mystical Hebrew text widely circulated among Jews during medieval times (also spelled cabala).

Koran: The sacred writing of the Islamic faith.

Reformation: The sixteenth and seventeenth century effort to reconstitute the Christian Church resulting in the separation of Protestantism from Roman Catholicism, especially through the leadership of Martin Luther and John Calvin.

Renaissance: The transitional movement in Europe between medieval and modern times beginning in Italy and marked by a humanistic revival of classical influence.

Sarcophagus: An ancient burial tomb.

Seraphim: Angelic beings mentioned in the Old Testament book of Isaiah as having six wings and standing at the side of the throne of God.

Sistrum: A kind of handheld musical noise maker used in ancient Egypt to ward off evil powers.

Talmud: An ancient collection of Rabbinical writings beyond the Old Testament scriptures that include the Mishnah and Gemara constituting the basis for religious authority within Judaism.

Walk to Emmaus: A 72-hour weekend experience of brief talks, group discussions, and worship sessions sponsored by the United Methodist Church in various parts of the country. It is ecumenical or interdenominational in attendance, open to all. It takes its origin from the Roman Catholic Cursillo movement and its name from the story of Jesus' appearance to the two disciples on the Road to Emmaus on the first Easter evening as recorded in Luke 24:13-35